Country House Estates

MARGARET WILLES

The National Trust

First published in 1996 by National Trust (Enterprises) Ltd
36 Queen Anne's Gate, London SW1H 9AS

© 1996 The National Trust
Registered Charity No. 205846
ISBN 0 7078 0246 6

A catalogue record for this book is available from the British Library

Text and picture research by Margaret Willes, Publisher, The National Trust

Designed by Peter Guy

Production by Bob Towell

Printed and bound in Hong Kong
Mandarin Offset Limited

Front cover: The walled garden and dovecote at Felbrigg, Norfolk
Title page: The arms of the Lucy family on the door of one of their carriages
at Charlecote Park, Warwickshire
Back cover: Edward Prince, carpenter at Erddig, Clwyd, in 1792;
a portrait by John Walters of Denbigh

Introduction

The text for this booklet, and for its companion volume (see page 48), has been adapted and expanded from the National Trust's Desk Diary for 1996, which took as its theme domestic arrangements in country houses. Here I am concentrating on the country-house estate – the realm of the land agent, the woodmen and gamekeepers, the stable lads and blacksmiths, the gardener and the laundrymaid.

Our own domestic arrangements have become so streamlined and relieved by machines that it is hard to imagine what life was like one hundred years ago, let alone five centuries back. To do the household wash, the laundrymaid would rise at two in the morning to heat up the copper, and washing day was an impossibly short concept – washing week was more the mark. A lawn would have to be trimmed by hand, the exotic fruit and flowers – so prized for the dinner table – would be raised lovingly in glasshouses heated by stoves that needed night-long stoking in the cold months. The list goes on.

The feedback that we get from visitors to National Trust houses is that they particularly enjoy seeing the kitchens, bathrooms and estate buildings. As most of us, if we were transported back into the past, would find ourselves on hands and knees weeding the knot garden rather than gazing down on it from a shady arbour, the overwhelming feeling must be of gratitude that we live in such convenient times. But studying the way a country-house estate was run also provides an excellent insight into history precisely because we do have a common experience.

I have drawn on National Trust guidebooks and Trust knowledge to pull together the threads for this booklet. Two houses stand out for the wealth of knowledge about their estates: Erddig in Clwyd, with its rich archives and unique series of servants' portraits; and Lyme Park in Cheshire, where memories of the estate staff were collected and recorded in *Cricketers Preferred* by Kedrun Laurie. Four books were particularly useful: *The Servants' Hall* by Merlin Waterson; *The English Country Estate* by John Martin Robinson; *The Art of Dining* by Sara Paston-Williams; and *Home Comfort* by Christina Hardyment. I am grateful to them all.

The Estate Yard

When Sir Robert Peel visited Woburn Abbey in Bedfordshire in 1849, he marvelled at the extent of the estate yard, declaring it 'more like a dockyard than a domestic office'. The yard, with its workshops, had become the centre of a large-scale enterprise, the result of the agricultural improvements made by landowners over the previous century.

A well-run estate was the duty of every patriot, as well as the basis of his political influence. As the 4th Earl of Bristol, of Ickworth, Suffolk, explained to the agricultural writer Arthur Young, 'I love agriculture because it makes good citizens . . . because it does not leave a man time to plunder his neighbours and because its plenty bereaves him of temptation' – precepts he did not adopt in his own rackety life.

To run these burgeoning enterprises, landowners employed professional managing agents, well grounded in agriculture and surveying. Different estates were organised in different ways, Lyme Park, home of the Legh family, on the borders of Cheshire, Derbyshire and Lancashire, was run very much in the typical 19th-century style. Lord Legh was responsible for all the farm buildings and cottages; his tenants for stocking and running those farms. His agent worked from a purpose-built estate office, assisted by a clerk of works and estate foreman. Through them he supervised the workshops in the estate yard – wagon sheds, smithy and sawmill – the woodlands, gardens and home farm. So keen were the Leghs on cricket that sporting prowess was an important criterion for employment. Sir Robert Peel's simile is echoed by the daughter of Mark Rawlinson, Lyme's clerk of works at the turn of this century: 'It was like being in a big hotel at Christmas, father used to say. But it was more like a factory when it came down to brass tacks.'

❧

A bird's-eye view of Charlecote Park in Warwickshire, painted by an unknown artist in 1696. Estate staff are shown working in the fields, while the Lucy family enjoy a picnic in the foreground

At Lanhydrock in Cornwall, a more modest estate, the managing agent was called the steward. From the 1850s until his retirement at the age of eighty-seven in 1908, the steward was the splendidly named Silvanus William Jenkin, who ran the immediate estate from a room inside the main house, while two offices at Liskeard and Redruth supervised the Robartes' eastern and western estates in the duchy. Under Jenkin came the home farm, stables, carpenters' shop, and the gardener's bothy; plus, as a sign of the times, the motor house and electrical generating plant.

Erddig in Clwyd not only has a splendid set of surviving estate workshops, but also detailed records of the people who worked in them. Erddig, just outside Wrexham, was the home of the Yorke family from 1733 until the house passed to the National Trust in 1973. The eldest Yorke sons were invariably called Simon or Philip, so were numbered to distinguish individuals. They enjoyed a particularly close relationship with their servants, commissioning a remarkable series of portraits, now hanging in the servants' hall, and writing poems about them. The original estate yard was built in the 1770s by Philip I; fifty years later Simon II built a new, larger estate yard, further from the main house, and this has survived more or less intact.

In the 1770s Erddig's estate was run for Philip I by his agent, John Caesar. A letter from Philip on 1 November 1770 gives an idea of the breadth of Caesar's responsibilities: from paying servants their board wages, the accounts of the mill, the behaviour of labourers, countering the threats of flooding, the sale of Philip's mare, to a message from Mrs Yorke concerning the amount of cheese in the house.

❧

The steward's room at Lanhydrock, Cornwall. Much of the furniture now in the room came from the Robartes' Liskeard office, which supervised the eastern Cornish estates.

A notice hanging in the agent's office at Erddig, Clwyd, urging staff to look out for trespassers on the estate, August 1826

In 1779 the head carpenter at Erddig was Edward Prince. He was comparatively highly paid, 1/6d per day as against the gardeners and gamekeepers, who received 10d. His portrait, painted in 1792, shows him with his tools, including a giant set of dividers. Also featured is a verse by Philip Yorke I:

> *A raiser this*, indeed of *Houses*,
> That has already had four Spouses;
> And if the present, don't survive,
> Hopes to rebuild them up, to five:

What the current Mrs Prince thought of this sentiment, history luckily does not relate.

In Simon II's time the carpenter was Thomas Rogers, who rose from pig boy to his position in the joiners' shop, now established in the new estate yard. His portrait shows him at work in the shop. Later in the 19th century, William Gittins combined the roles of carpenter and estate foreman, with twelve men working under him. His skills ranged from building new cottages, repairing walls and roads, to making fences and re-roofing. The skilled house joinery was undertaken by John Jones, but Gittins made the toy train for Simon IV, still to be seen in the nursery at Erddig.

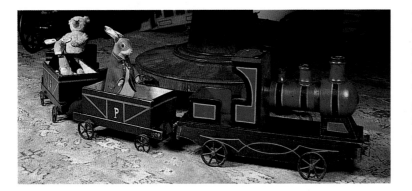

Thomas Rogers, carpenter at Erddig in the 19th century. This portrait, commissioned by Simon II Yorke from an unknown artist in 1830, shows Rogers at his work bench. He was lucky to be there, for in 1815, while working on estate cottages at Plas Grono, he was press-ganged and Simon had to rescue him by paying ransom for his release

The toy train made by William Gittins, estate carpenter at Erddig, for Simon IV Yorke's fifth birthday in 1908

A blacksmith's shop was also included in the 1830's estate yard at Erddig. This was the workplace at the turn of this century of Joseph Wright, whose versatile skills were recorded in Philip II's poem of 1911:

> He fits for use by various arts
> Our waggons, implements and carts;
> Cyclests who here a visit pay
> Go forth rejoicing on their way
> Our engine and hydraulic rams
> Our tanks and taps and water dams
> And locks and keys and hinges too.

In the 18th century, Erddig was famous for its beechwoods which drew a compliment from 'Farmer' George III. In 1830 the woodman was Edward Barnes, whose portrait also hangs in the servants' hall. Timber would be drawn to the estate yard in the wood waggon, which still stands in its shed. Originally the timber was sawn up in the two-man pit next to the joiners' shop, but in the later 19th century, when a lot of heavy machinery had been introduced into the yard, it was passed through the sawmill, powered by a steam engine. Machines were replacing men, and, like many household offices, the estate yard was facing extinction.

❧

The estate yard at Killerton, Devon, c. 1925, showing workmen in front of the sawmill. In the 1930s there were 150 horses regularly shod at the blacksmith's shop

The Stables

Until the coming of the motor car in the early 20th century, horses played a vital role in the life of the country-house estate. This importance is reflected in the stable block, which was often as grand as the main house. Perhaps the most grandiose National Trust example is the mid-Victorian stable-block built by H. H. Kendall at Wimpole Hall, Cambridgeshire, the entrance crowned by an enormous clock turret.

By the 18th century, the stables were usually run by the head coachman, who supervised the maintenance of the horses and the carriages. He also had to be a skilled horseman – driving coaches could be a dangerous occupation, though the coachman at Erddig in the 1850s may well have been accident prone, as he was described in the Yorke verse as 'clumsy alike in form and walk' and seriously injured himself climbing on to a coach. The grooms fed and cared for the horses, accompanying the master or mistress when they went riding. The postilion would ride one of the carriage horses and thus be able to control them if they took fright.

All these servants wore a special uniform called livery, provided by their employer and usually picking out the family colours, to emphasise dignity and status. At Erddig, Philip Yorke I kept a detailed record of the hiring of his stable staff in his personal pocket book: 'May 24 1776. Agreed with my coachman Ambrose Campion, who came to my service this day, as follows, to give him 20£ a year wages, a full suit of livery with plush breeches, l pr Buckskin breeches, Waistcoat and Frock Great coat, and boots in every second year, and to provide himself out of his said wages with a frock coat for common work. Allow him also a jacket when neat.' Examples of frock great coats provided for the coachmen still hang in the butler's pantry at Erddig.

A negro postilion resplendently dressed in scarlet and blue livery with silver braid and buttons. The portrait hangs in the servants' hall at Erddig and tradition identifies him as the coachboy to John Meller, owner of the estate in the early 18th century

Of the Conditions of this Negro,
Our information is but moore,
However here, he was a dweller,
And blew the horn for Master Mell....
Here, too he dy'd, but when or ho....
Can scarcely be remember'd now....
But that to Marchwiel he was s....
And had good Christian interment....
Pray Heavn may stand his present fri....
Where black, or white, distinctions, en....
For sure on this side of the grav....
They are too strong, twixt Lord & Sla....
Here also liv'd a dingy brother,
Who play'd together with the oth....
But of him, yet longer rotten....
Every particular's forgotten....
Save that like Tweedle-dum & d....
These bat in notes, could e'er agre....
In all things else, as they do tell....
Were just like Handel and Corell....
O had it been in their life's course....
I have met with Massa Wilber force....
They wou'd in this alone, have join....
And been together of a mind,....
Have rais'd their horns, to one high ....
And blown his Merits, to the Moo....

The Harpur Crewe family of Calke Abbey in Derbyshire were particularly attached to their horses. No sooner had Sir John Harpur finished his grand baroque mansion in the opening years of the 18th century, than he turned his attention to the matter of the stables. William Gilkes, master builder, created a detached quadrangular stable block to the west of the main house. On the ground floor there are stalls for horses, separated by stout columns on supporting arcades, the tack room for storing saddles and horse trappings, the smithy and the coach-house with its wide doors. Above are the granaries and hayloft, and accommodation for the staff.

Sir John also introduced one of the first Arab stallions, the 'Harpur Arabian', into the country and established a stud at Calke. His enthusiasm for racehorses was inherited by his grandson, Sir Harry, who in the late 1760s commissioned Joseph Pickford of Derby to build a riding school so that his horses might exercise in inclement weather. In 1777, however, the racehorse establishment was transferred to another Harpur property, Swarkestone, adjoining Derby Racecourse. Sir Harry also commissioned paintings of his favourite horses, which now hang on the staircase and in the library at Calke.

Sir Vauncey Harpur Crewe, master of Calke from 1886 until 1924, refused to allow motor cars to enter the park. As a result of this resolute determination, the house has a fine collection of carriages. The three types of coachman-driven carriage in general use in the 19th century – brougham, victoria and landau – are all represented, together with owner-driven vehicles like the phaeton and the ralli.

✥℘

The stables at Kedleston, Derbyshire (not currently open to the public). Similar in scale to those at neighbouring Calke Abbey, they were designed by Samuel Wyatt when he was clerk of works to the estate in the 1760s. Twenty horses were accommodated in fine vaulted surroundings, each with its own stall, hay manger and name plate

At Arlington Court in Devon, there is another good collection of carriages, this time gathered together rather than inherited with the house. The earliest example is a travelling carriage that belonged to the Marquis of Anglesey at the beginning of the 19th century. This vehicle was used for long journeys, including the Grand Tour. It would have had a postilion and the horses would have been changed at regular posting places. A sword case was thoughtfully provided at the back, accessible only from the interior of the carriage.

In 1840 Mary Elizabeth Lucy of Charlecote Park in Warwickshire, set off on a European tour, along with her husband George, the tutor, a courier, a nurse, five children, a new-born baby and the footman. Their transport consisted of two carriages, a coach and a chariot. Mary Elizabeth noted in her diary the luggage, which included '3 beds for the little ones, 3 tin baths, sheets, towels, pillows, and we had a sort of well fixed under the coach which held lesson books, tea, arrowroot and every possible thing we thought we might need'. Luckily a sword was never required, though the journey was a tragic one, with two of the children dying en route.

By the beginning of the 20th century time was already running out for horse, carriage and the country-house stables. At Lyme Park the coachman learned to drive the new, horseless carriage just before the First World War. As Reg Feltham, electrician, hall porter and park keeper, recalled, 'When they bought the car, that was the end of Lyme. When the horses left, the wheelwright and the blacksmith left, and the "village" started to disintegrate.'

❦

The tack room at Charlecote Park, where saddlery and other riding equipment was kept clean and stored

The Gardener's Bothy

In the 19th century at Chatsworth in Derbyshire, it was said that the two most important people were the 6th Duke of Devonshire and his gardener, Joseph Paxton. The Duke once wrote to Paxton, 'I had rather all the flowers in the garden were dead than you ill'.

Of all the staff of a country-house estate, the most difficult to define in status is the head gardener, for he plays a different role in every household. In some he is a figure of considerable prestige – Joseph Paxton was, of course, exceptional, but there are others whose relationship with their employer was more like a partnership, such as that between the Messel family and James Comber at Nymans in Sussex. At Biddulph Grange in Staffordshire, however, the fact that James Bateman and his wife Maria were keen gardeners and skilled at horticultural tasks means that their head gardeners are not well documented. At times, the head gardener could rule as a tyrant in his realm of herbaceous borders and hot houses, at others he was a subservient figure, answerable to the clerk of works or estate foreman.

From the 18th century, the main task of the head gardener was to provide fresh fruit, vegetables and flowers for the house. Glasshouses had been added to houses from the 17th century, at first to grow oranges and lemons, with warmth supplied by braziers. Later, conservatories, pits and frames heated by stoves were built for the cultivation of tender flowers and exotic fruits, including that symbol of Georgian gastronomic one-upmanship, pineapples.

❧

The Victorian orangery at Peckover House in Wisbech, Cambridgeshire. The orange trees are reputed to be more than three hundred years old

Calke Abbey provides a good example of a late-Georgian garden. The main purpose of the seven acres of walled garden was to contribute to the domestic economy of the estate by providing fruit and vegetables all the year round. The Physic Garden sounds as if it was run to grow medicinal herbs, but it was in fact a kitchen garden, with a stove-house built in 1785 and a vinery added twenty years later, together with pits and frames for growing cucumbers, melons, pineapples and violets. In the 1830s the head gardener at Calke was John Vernon, assisted by a staff of seven men and, unusually, three women. Vernon's headquarters was the bothy, approached along a path flanked by sweet peas and dahlias. It still contains the 18th-century fittings, including seed cabinets with innumerable small drawers.

In some households the garden bothy was the communal living area for the young lads working in the garden. At Lyme Park at the turn of this century, three boys shared it as their bedroom, with meals brought in for them. Young lads started their working life in their early teens. James Comber was a farmer's son, who, from an early age, was fascinated by horticulture, sending off for his first packet of Sutton seeds at the age of nine. Gardening offered excellent prospects even for those from a modest background, as every estate had its gardeners, and the head gardener of an aristocratic estate could gain considerable prestige. In 1879, aged thirteen, Comber began his career at Wakehurst Place in Sussex, working from 6am to 5.30pm six days a week and earning 5s. Working his way up, he moved from 'improver' to journeyman, and at the age of 29 secured the post of head gardener at Nymans with Ludwig Messel. He stayed with the Messels for the rest of his life, helping to build up the great collection of plants at Nymans, and dying full of horticultural honours in 1953.

❧

The interior of the gardener's bothy at Calke Abbey, painted blue to drive away flies. Each drawer in the 18th-century cabinet is assigned to a different vegetable

Head gardeners were usually given their own house – at Nymans, Comber's delightful Garden Cottage, covered in roses and honeysuckle, can still be seen. But some establishments frowned on the idea of the gardener having his own household. Advertisements in *The Gardeners' Chronicle* often carried the admonition, 'no incumbents'; Joseph Addison, head gardener to the Leghs at Lyme Park from 1907 to 1922, counted himself lucky that no mention was made of his five children at his interview.

Thomas Pritchard, head gardener at Erddig, had his portrait painted in 1830 outside his house, which still stands at one end of the kitchen garden, conveniently near the greenhouses. The Yorkes didn't worry about 'incumbents' either, for Simon II wrote a verse in his honour, complimenting him on his family:

> He shone more bright in Marriage State,
> And raised young plants from teaming Mate.

His successor was James Phillips, a conservative soul according to the Yorkes:

> Old-fashioned, in his notions, he
> With foreign names did not agree
> "Quatre-Saisons" "Quarter-Sessions" meant,
> The "Bijou" as "By Joe" went
> "Glory to die John" was the Rose,
> Which each as "Gloire de Dijon" knows.
> No Green-house here 'twas his advice
> The Antique Frames would well suffice.

❧

Thomas Pritchard, head gardener at Erddig, depicted outside his house with his cat and top hat. When this portrait was painted in 1830, he was sixty-seven, and described by Simon II Yorke as 'old and run to seed'. In his youth he had worked alongside the gamekeeper, Jack Henshaw, portrayed on page 43

The running of hothouses, kitchen gardens and herbaceous borders was a labour-intensive exercise, and so the number of gardeners employed could be large. At Petworth in Sussex at the beginning of this century the Egremonts employed twenty gardeners (the National Trust now looks after the gardens with four). At the same time at Nymans, James Comber had twelve people to help him, while at Melford Hall in Suffolk in the 1930s, the head gardener, Mr Pomfret had only four gardeners and a boy. Perhaps this explains why he was such an irascible character. Ulla, Lady Hyde-Parker recalled: 'I don't think I ever saw a smile on his face, or his eyes light up. It was Pomfret's dress which gave one a feeling that he was of importance, for he always wore a black bowler hat, a green baize apron covering the front of his black trousers and jacket, and a white shirt.'

The relationship between the country-house garden and the kitchen was naturally close. Every morning the head gardener would leave baskets of fresh fruit and vegetables at the kitchen door for the cook. It was also the head gardener's job to arrange the flowers in the house. At Melford, Pomfret cut the greenhouse flowers, brought them into the various rooms by 10am and arranged them. The first priority was the dining-room table, with eight crystal vases filled with the finest carnations, orchids or whatever was in season at the time. Neither the mistress of the house nor the butler had a say in the flowers, or in the fruit piled in beautiful pyramids on the sideboard. As at P. G. Wodehouse's Blandings Castle, where the head gardener, Angus McAllister, tyrannised Lord Emsworth, so at Melford Hall, Pomfret 'reigned supreme'.

The walled kitchen garden at Felbrigg, Norfolk (see also page 45), showing Wyken Pippin, one of the early varieties of apples grown as espaliers against the walls

Forcing pots in the kitchen garden at Felbrigg

[24]

The Laundry

With modern automatic washing machines, or public launderettes at hand, it is virtually impossible to imagine the long and laborious process once involved in laundrywork. Many people can remember the washing day of their youth – damp, steamy, inconvenient - but in the heyday of the great house a day was by no means sufficient to get through the vast piles of laundry: it was a continuous process. A glance at the inventory of linen at Shugborough in Shropshire in 1792 conveys the size of the task: from 85 damask tablecloths, through 92 dozen table napkins to 17 pairs of holland sheets and 24 pairs of servants' sheets. On top of this there were all the clothes of the family, often involving complex frills and ruffs, and the servants' clothes, including heavily soiled items from gardeners and stablemen.

The laundry has traditionally been women's work, even in the Middle Ages when the household servants were almost exclusively male. Sometimes the laundry would be sent out to professional 'whitsters', or they were hired to come in on set days to do the washing. If a country house had its own laundry, it was traditionally sited near the stables, to keep the pungent smells away from the main body of the house and to give access to drying and bleaching grounds. In the 19th century, however, concern was expressed at the unholy alliances that might be forged between the laundrymaid and the stableboy, and Victorian laundries tend to be sited near or within the mansion.

The laundry was composed of three principal parts: the wash house, the drying loft or closet, and the laundry room for pressing and ironing. On fine days the clothes would be spread out in the adjoining fields or special walled gardens, planted with sweet-smelling bushes like lavender and rosemary to scent the linen and clothes.

The laundry at Petworth, Sussex, in the 1870s. This print is part of a remarkable collection of 19th-century photographs taken by the Wyndhams of their servants and household offices. Airing racks loaded with household linen have been hoisted to the ceiling, and other wooden racks on the floor are festooned with clothes. The old lady on the left is using a flat iron

The wash-house, usually called the wet laundry, would have a high ceiling to allow the steam to escape, and a channelled floor to ensure drainage. A lead cistern would be located nearby to provide soft rainwater. Equipment within the wet laundry included wooden washing troughs and tubs, or bucks, and a built-in copper, filled and emptied with dippers and buckets, and heated by a fire beneath. The laundrymaid would rise at 2am or 3am on washdays to get the fire lit and the coppers going.

Clothes and linen were cleaned by soaking in an alkaline solution called lye, made from wood or bracken or fern ash dissolved in water. The tub or buck had a spigot in its base. The lye would be poured over the clothes, and the process repeated until the water through the spigot came out clear. Heavily stained clothes could be boiled in the copper after soaking in lye. Soap provided a more expensive alternative, but there were competing household priorities for the animal fat which made up its main constituent: for cooking and making candles. For treatments to spots and stains, a book published in 1582 provides some delicate localised solutions: for grease and oil, an absorbent powder like fuller's earth or ground sheeps' trotters; for ink and iron stains, citrus juice; for stained lace, urine or ale.

The original washing-machine was a hand-held dolly, a wooden implement like a multi-legged stool, twisted to force the soapy water through the clothes. In 1861 the first rotary machine was produced, with an octagonal outer case and circular drum rotated by a wheel. This machine was called a Vowel and the models developed from A to U: Mrs Beeton recommended the E in her 1883 *Manual*, and Erddig has an example of an I. The first machine with an electric motor was introduced from the United States in the early 20th century, and the laundry at Berrington Hall, Hereford and Worcester, has a Thor cylinder machine from the 1920s.

The wet laundry at Erddig showing one of the copper boilers, together with a zinc dolly tub, wooden dolly and scoops. On the left is a hand-geared, two-roller mangle

The dry laundry, usually next door to the wet room, would accommodate the equipment for drying and pressing. In the dry laundries at Berrington and Erddig there are drying closets, brick enclosures over water-heating furnaces, with iron frames that slide in and out. For pressing there would be a long steady table or folding board. The mangle was there not for wringing, but for ironing large flat linen such as tablecloths and sheets. An example of an 18th-century box mangle is to be found at Shugborough, the box contained stones to apply weight while the damp linen passed through the rollers. Pressing of smaller items was done with irons, either box or flat. The box-irons were kept hot by filling the box with heated slugs of metal, the flat-irons would be heated directly on a stove. The mid-19th-century laundry at Castle Ward in Northern Ireland has a special stove that could heat up several irons simultaneously. They would be of different sizes, and include cap, Italian and goffering machines to undertake the skilled pressing of lace cuffs, tucks, and so on. The upper laundrymaid would usually handle the family's fine linen, including the delicate ironing, while the household washing was undertaken by an undermaid.

Given the large amount of articles passing through the laundry, lists were kept, usually by the housekeeper. In some houses there was a sorting room to keep track: Robert Kerr, author of *The Gentleman's House*, 1864, recommended that it should be fitted up with bins for different classifications of clothes. These would then be transferred to the laundry in separate wicker baskets. The washing and ironing processes over, the housekeeper would check the linen against her list before storing it in cupboards in her room, while maids and valets would return the appropriate items of clothing to their owners. Nevertheless, the lost sock syndrome must have been a fairly common occurrence.

The dry laundry at Beningbrough, Yorkshire. In the middle of the room there is a box mangle to press large items of laundry like sheets and tablecloths. To the left of the boiler there are two early 20th-century hand-operated washing machines.

Irons and other equipment in the dry laundry at Castle Ward, County Down

[30]

The Brewhouse and the Bakehouse

In a letter written in 1815, Sir Henry Harpur of Calke Abbey fulminated: 'As to the Baker, I caution you against any consultation with him. He is the man who has spoiled all my beer for the last year . . . he is neither a good baker nor a good Brewer.' The processes of brewing and baking were closely linked, both requiring malt and other grains, and yeast. Often the two establishments shared a chimney stack, fuel store and grain loft: sometimes, as at Calke, they were managed by the same person.

In the Middle Ages the universal drink was ale brewed from barley. Festivities would be called church ales, christening ales, and so on. In the 16th century hops were introduced from Flanders for the manufacture of beer, to the intense disapproval of patriots like Dr Andrew Boorde, author of *A Dyetary of Helth* published in 1542: 'Beere is a Dutch boorish liquor, a thing not known in England, till of late days an Alien to our Nation, till such times as Hops and Heresies came against us.' But the preservative quality of hops meant that beer gradually prevailed.

Fear of disease and pollution meant that water was not drunk, so beer and ale were taken at every meal. At the Earl of Northumberland's Sussex home, Petworth, in the 16th century, barley was grown on the estate, while hops were bought in. Brewing usually took place in March and October when the weather was neither too hot nor too cold. Single or small beer was provided for the household, double or strong beer for the Earl and his family.

❧

Sixteenth-century painted glass in the King's Room, Oxburgh Hall, Norfolk, showing the brewing of ale

One of the earliest surviving country-house brewhouses is at Lacock Abbey in Wiltshire, built by Sir William Sharington in the mid-16th century. It lies on the north side of the quadrangle of domestic buildings, next to the bakehouse. A flight of steps leads to the massive copper, where the water was boiled and cooled until the brewster could see his face on the surface of the liquid. The liquid was then run off into the mash tun and the malt added to produce a sweet extract, wort. This was reboiled in the copper with hops and sugar, and again run off, this time into the fermenting tun of oak staves with iron rings. Yeast was added, and the beer strained into casks.

When the Anson family decided to make their estate of Shugborough more or less self-sufficient in the 18th century, they built not only a brewhouse but also included a malt-house in the nearby model home farm. As in Elizabethan times, the beer and ale at Shugborough were brewed to different strengths. The top quality, drunk exclusively by the Anson family at dinner, was 'strong, very old' and named Old Tom after Thomas Anson, squire from 1720 to 1773. The second quality was 'ale' for family and servants; the third, 'beer', with an alcoholic content of two to three per cent, was drunk by servants throughout the day, apart from their main meal, when they were given ale.

The growth of commercial brewers led to a decline of country-house brewing in the 19th century. Bucking the trend, however, was Henry Dryden, known as the Antiquary, of Canons Ashby in Northamptonshire. In the 1860s he brewed his own beer, with bicarbonate of soda to add extra fizz, and then went out into the byways dressed as a tramp to invite travellers home to sample his brew.

❧

The Tudor brewhouse at Lacock Abbey, Wiltshire, showing the copper, mash and fermenting tuns, and the cooling trough

In the Middle Ages quality and type of bread were determined by the flour used. Wheat produced the finest, whitest bread, a rare luxury: this type was sometimes known as paindemain, from *panis dominis*, lord's bread, and would have graced only the high table. Torte, bread made from coarsely ground wheat flour, was baked in flat loaves for use as trenchers, or bread plates. Most bread was made from a mixture of grains. Maslin bread, from *miscelin*, Norman French for mixture, often contained wheat, rye and barley; this was the bread consumed by household servants.

In medieval and Tudor times bread would usually be baked in an oven built into the wall of the chimney-breast of the great kitchen hearth. In the 1520s kitchen at Compton Castle in Devon, for instance, there are two bread ovens set into the massive, 15-feet wide fireplace. Free-standing bread ovens were first built in the 16th century, often in separate bakehouses to cut down the hazard of fire. At Charlecote the 18th-century bakehouse stood next door to the brewhouse and provided access to the fires under its coppers. In the Erddig bakehouse, also dating from the 18th century, visitors today can watch the process of breadmaking. The dough is mixed in a wooden trough, often called an ark. The lid is then closed and sacks put on top to get the dough to rise. The lid can also be used for rolling out and kneading the dough.

❧

The 16th-century cornmill at Nether Alderley, Cheshire, powered by water from the manorial pond

From the bread oven built into the chimney-breast through to separate bakehouse, the principles of baking remained the same. The oven would be of brick, circular or tunnel-like depending on size, with a domed roof to radiate heat evenly. Faggots of furze and blackthorn, or wood splinters tied into bundles, were placed in the oven and lit to provide an intense heat. In an age before thermometers, the baker would judge the temperature by using pebbles that changed colour at a certain heat. Once this temperature was achieved the ashes were scraped out and the bread slid in on a long wooden paddle or peel. The mouth of the oven was stopped by a flat stone (later by an iron door) and sealed with wet clay. A clever baker could use his cooling oven to cook a whole series of dishes: bread required the most intense heat; next came rich pies, patties and pastries; as the oven continued to cool milk puddings and custards could be baked slowly in specially turned wooden dishes.

As with the brewhouse, the country-house bakehouse declined with the advent of the commercial bakery. One of the last bakehouses to be built was at Lanhydrock in the 1880s, complete with an elaborate bread oven from the doyen of manufacturers, Clement, Jeakes & Co of Bloomsbury in London.

❦

The bakehouse at Lanhydrock, built after the 1881 fire. The bread oven, supplied by Clement, Jeakes & Co., takes four days to heat to a steady temperature

Fish, Fur & Feathers

'No man need ever have an ill-provisioned house if there be but attached to it a dovecot, a warren and a fish-pond', wrote Olivier de Serres in 1603. When roads were poor and markets scarce, country estates had to be as self-sufficient as possible.

Fish formed an important part of the diet in medieval England: Wednesdays, Fridays and Saturdays were ordained by the Church as meatless, and thus fish days, as were the forty days of Lent. Even after the Reformation fish days were continued by command of Elizabeth I to support the fishing industry.

Away from the coast, supplies of fresh fish for the table meant keeping fish-ponds or stews. Monasteries like Fountains Abbey in Yorkshire would have three freshwater ponds: pike in the first; less predatory fish in the second; and fish ready for the table in the third. Secular estates also had their stews: late-Elizabethan household accounts of the Northumberland family at Petworth in Sussex and of Bess of Hardwick in Derbyshire include references to men who maintained the ponds and caught the fish for the clerk of the kitchen.

Richard Carew of Antony House in Cornwall was a fish fanatic. In 1610 he built a small house on his estate to prepare fishy feasts, and wrote a piscatorial poem, beginning

> My fishful pond is my delight
> There sucking mullet, swallowing bass
> Side-walking crab, wry-mouthed fluke
> and slip-fast eel, as evenings pass

Fishing was becoming a sport for gentlemen. On one of the lakes at Kedleston Hall in Derbyshire, Robert Adam built a delightful pavilion in the early 1770s. Intrepid anglers could set out for fishing expeditions from one of its two boat-houses, while the ladies cast their lines out of its window, safely protected from the sun. By the late 18th century most country-house fish-ponds had either been filled in or merged as picturesque features into the landscape. The development of transporting fresh fish packed with ice meant that this particular kind of larder was no longer vital.

❧

The fishing pavilion at Kedleston, a combination of fishing room, boat-house and cold plunge bath designed in 1769 by Robert Adam for Lord Scarsdale

Deer-parks and rabbit warrens provided the Norman kings and their followers with two of their great pleasures: the chase and the table. Fallow deer were introduced by the Normans as they were easy to keep enclosed and by the 14th century there were over 3,000 parks in England. These were all licensed by the Crown and subject to fierce game laws: these laws were to remain in force in varying degrees for different offences over the centuries, ensuring that the gamekeeper and his staff had an enduring tenure in the households of country estates.

The history of Black Park at Chirk, on the borders of Wales and England, reflects the rise and fall of the deer-park. In the early 14th century 460 acres of wasteland were enclosed by the Mortimers as a hunting park, and household accounts refer to the keeping of the lord's greyhound bitch and eight puppies, and the lord's nine sparrowhawks. At this time venison enjoyed a special status in the kitchen, usually exchanged as gifts, often in pasties. Three centuries later, Sir Thomas Myddelton extended the park to hold 500 deer, but by 1770 the last forty animals were given away. By this time, gentlemen were finding the pleasures of the hunt elsewhere, and the deer-parks that remained were transformed into landscape arcadias.

The fate of the rabbit warren is similar. Rabbit meat was much prized for the table, and special 'coning earths', mounds that protected the rabbits from predators, were built. The Northumberland accounts for 1349 refer to repairs to the palings and gates of the earths, and to the purchase of tar to preserve trunks of trees from the nibbling rodents. There is an area of the Petworth estate still called the Cony Park. But by the late 18th century land was required for agriculture and rabbits were being treated by gamekeepers as vermin rather than as animals to conserve for the table.

Jack Henshaw, gamekeeper at Erddig: a portrait painted in 1791 by John Walters of Denbigh as part of a series for Philip I Yorke. The accompanying verse by Philip describes Henshaw as a 'lover true to fur and feather'

Æt. 59

Goes doth here attempt to draw
That best of Beaters — Jack Wallis
A setter true, to fur, and feather
Who tired not, nor lost his leather
Near forty years, through bush, and bry,
He beated for the elder Squire,
Who now together with his gun,
Hath made him over to his son
Long may he reign with pole and bagg,
And never, in the Cover, flagg,
Sink his faculties, in strong October,
Nor at night, go home, too sober.

The dovecote could provide a source of fresh pigeon meat and eggs throughout the winter months, and thus was a highly prized component of the estate. In addition, the birds' dung was a good fertiliser, and could be used in tanning and the manufacture of gunpowder. Pigeon down and feathers filled pillows and bolsters. By the late 17th century it was calculated that there were 26,000 dovecotes in Britain, accommodating approximately 250,000 birds – eating grain that would otherwise have fed 100,000 people.

The National Trust owns a whole variety of dovecotes. Some are free-standing – like the stone dome that sits discreetly in the grounds at Cotehele in Cornwall, next to the fish-ponds, or the magnificent half-timbered structure at Hawford in Worcestershire. Others are part of another structure – like Willington in Bedfordshire, where accommodation for 1,500 birds sits atop the 16th-century stables, or the monks' great barn at Buckland Abbey in Devon, where the lofts are sited in the projecting porches. Some are just delightful landscape features – the cote at Felbrigg in Norfolk has 'therm' windows, redolent of a Roman bath, while the slim dove tower at Chirk, Clwyd, sports romantic battlements. By the time these last examples were built, agricultural innovations made it possible to keep cattle and sheep through the winter, and so the need to keep pigeons for food was a romantic gesture rather than a vital necessity.

❧

The dovecote in the middle of the walled garden at Felbrigg. It was built in 1753 for William Windham II, possibly by James Paine who used the same motif of therm, or Roman bath, windows in the house

The range of wild birds taken for the table in the Middle Ages was huge – including those we would now find unacceptable, such as herons and bitterns, and others that have become extinct, such as the bustard. These birds would have been taken with falcons or hawks as sport, or netted by the household's fowler to supply the kitchen. Partridges and pheasants were often raised as domesticated birds in the poultry-yard. The mid-16th-century Petre household accounts for Ingatestone Hall in Essex mention an enclosure running along the orchard wall to protect partridges and pheasants alongside turkeys. But these same accounts also give an early reference to the use of gunpowder to shoot wild fowl: a development that was eventually to transform the killing of game-birds from provision for the table to sport on a huge scale.

By the early 19th century, improved shooting techniques combined with the increasing practice of beating flying birds over the guns meant that birds could be shot in quantity. Open seasons were instituted, forming part of the social calendar: grouse in August; partridges after harvest; pheasants from October to Christmas. Some estates, especially those in the north, were now run entirely for their game and shooting. At Penrhyn Castle in North Wales, Lord and Lady Penrhyn were in residence only for the shooting season. The sporting interests were put in the hands of the head-keeper, Andrew Foster, who had a staff of eight. Five hundred brace of grouse and 3,000 pheasants were reared annually. All this had a huge effect on the size of bags: in the late 18th century the number of birds shot annually was counted in hundreds; a hundred years later, thousands were killed during a weekend.

❧

The massed bodies of pheasants, with one hare, that made up the day's bag for a shoot at Saltram in Devon, November 1894. The Morley family, guests and gamekeepers proudly look on

Household Management

A companion to this booklet, concentrating on the realm of the housekeeper, the butler,
the cook and the nursery maids.